Y0-EJL-362

Making Nuclear War Impossible

MAKING NUCLEAR WAR IMPOSSIBLE

Howard S. Brembeck

News Printing Company, Inc. 1984

Making Nuclear War Impossible

Copyright © 1984, by Howard S. Brembeck

All rights reserved: This book may not be reproduced in whole or in part, without permission. Inquiries should be addressed to the **Alternative World Foundation, Inc.** AWF-1, Goshen, Indiana 46526

Published by:

News Printing Company, Inc.
114 S. Main Street
Goshen, Indiana 46526

PRINTED IN THE UNITED STATES OF AMERICA
First Edition

*"All the problems of the world
could be settled easily,
if men were only willing to think."*
— Nicholas Murray Butler

*"The less men think . . .
the more they talk."*
— Montesquieu

DEDICATION

This book is dedicated to all who have contributed to my life.

Howard S. Brembeck

CONTENTS

I.	An Unprecedented World Problem	15
II.	The Search for the Alternative	23
III.	Thoughtful Judgments	35
IV.	The Alternative Defense Plan	49
V.	The Challenge	67
VI.	Victory Strategy	77
VII.	Life Assurance	105
VIII.	The Land of the Free and The Home of the Brave	113
IX.	Living in The Alternative World	121

FORWARD

We are living in a "talk" age surrounded by machines (telephone, radio, television, and computers) that are constantly talking to us. We attend meetings of all kinds just for talking. Some feel we can solve all our problems with talk. Possibly we have an obsession with talk. If this be true and the men quoted are right, does it not follow that we may be looking in the wrong place for the answers to our problems?

Making Nuclear War Impossible, we believe, could be the answer to our present world nuclear problem. It shows how economic power can be used to nullify military power, to make aggression so unprofitable that offensive weaponry would be of no practical use, and how nuclear and other mass life-exterminating weaponry can be eliminated without the loss of sovereign power to any nation. It also gives you a peek into THE ALTERNATIVE WORLD, which would be the period following the "Alternative Defense Plan" — the time when all people can live at a much higher level.

In this small book we make no attempt to go into technicalities, but rather present a broad overview of the "Alternative Defense Plan."

> The Alternative World Foundation is a nonprofit, completely independent (no ties to any organization of any kind) public corporation. It is managed by a Board of Directors consisting of leaders in business, education and religion.

ALTERNATIVE WORLD FOUNDATION, INC.
AWF-1
803 N. MAIN STREET
GOSHEN, INDIANA 46526

Making Nuclear War Impossible

CHAPTER I

An Unprecedented World Problem

"To create a problem and not correct it creates an even greater problem."

— *Confucius*

I

An Unprecedented World Problem

In 1945, by creating an atomic-powered weapon, the United States brought to the world a problem unlike any it had previously faced. It might have been expected that having the imagination and energy to create such a devastating weapon, it would also have the intelligence and discipline to control or remove it. This has not been the case.

Making Nuclear War Impossible

As a consequence, the United States is now having to create more nuclear weapons to protect itself against the offspring of the original bomb which has been embraced and multiplied by its adversary and other nations.

If you continue to feed a tiger, eventually he will eat you as well."

— *Chinese proverb*

The problem facing the United States and other nations that have embraced nuclear weaponry is how to give it sanctuary without being consumed by it. It's like living permanently in the same room with a man-eating tiger. At first, you have him chained in a corner where he cannot reach you or others. Since you cannot escape from the room, realistically you know that eventually the tiger will break his chain and eat you.

An Unprecedented World Problem

Some think it is possible to live safely in this world with nuclear weapons under arms control agreements. AWF (the Alternative World Foundation) does not. It contends that it is easier to eliminate nuclear weapons than to control them and that we possess the power to destroy anything we create. All that is needed is the will.

It might be possible for man to live with nuclear weapons were they God like creatures, but all men are not reasonable rational beings. Many are more prone to emotion than reason, more attracted to rumor than fact, and periodically are subject to spasms of insane behavior. If men were sane animals they would not have the armament problem they do today.

Therefore we must conclude; that as long as nuclear weapons exist, there is the con-

Making Nuclear War Impossible

stant danger they will be used. But we are confident that men have the intelligence and reason to devise a feasible way to erase them from the earth. For simplicity's sake we call this way the "ALTERNATIVE".

CHAPTER II

The Search For The Alternative

"Merely ignoring a problem will not make it go away . . . Nor will merely recognizing it."

— Cullen Hightower

II

The Search For The Alternative

"There is a way — find it."
— Thomas Edison

Realizing nuclear weapons are an enormous threat to human existence, the United States has promoted arms control talks with the Soviet Union. But merely talking about arms, rather than having the expected effect

Making Nuclear War Impossible

of limiting or reducing the amount of arms, has had the opposite effect. Arms control talks have become a stage for each nation to expound its propaganda and attempt to influence other nations.

If talks between the USA and the USSR continue to focus on arms rather than mutually desirable, long-range goals, inevitably this will lead to nuclear war. Never in the history of the world has there been a confrontation of the magnitude that now exists between the United States and Russia. Realistically, a state of war already exists. This can be seen on the perimeters of the spheres of influence. We are caught in a war between two economic and two political, incompatible ideologies. Economically, we have Karl Marx warring against Adam Smith. Politically, we have Lenin and Stalin warring

The Search for the Alternative

against the men who founded our nation. To this we must add the fact that technologically our world is now one nation, and the two superpowers in confrontation are warring for control of the world nation. If either attains a definite armament advantage over the other that can be exploited politically or militarily, it could subject the other nation to its rule and establish a world government to which all nations could be made accountable.

Returning to our search to avoid the seemingly inevitable, let us first evaluate the two economic theories of these nations. In the 60 years that Russia has embraced Marxism, it has had the opportunity to prove its value. Instead it has proved that it doesn't work. However, through propaganda it has convinced many people in many nations that it does work and that capitalism is a decadent economic practice. Ironically, capitalism has for 60 years been supporting Marxism from the fruits of its enterprise.

We see the primary basis for the confrontation between the USA and the USSR as economic. Consequently, our search for ways to avoid a nuclear confrontation involves trying to figure out how to use our nonviolent strength, our economic power, for example, to persuade the Soviet Union to join us in eliminating nuclear and other mass life-exterminating offensive weapons.

Alongside the economic study we studied the beliefs and principles of the men who founded the United States and the men who founded the Soviet Union. Here we find a startling difference, with roots that go back thousands of years. Not only are we im-

The Search for the Alternative

pressed with the intellectual superiority of the men who founded the United States, but we are overcome with a sense of unworthiness, or guilt, for not having held as firmly to their beliefs as the Russians hold to the beliefs of the men who established their government.

A third difference arises from our study of the Russians. It, too, is startling, and we believe must be taken into account in any plan for effectively cooling off and reducing the USA-USSR arms confrontation. The Russians' historical background, type of government, way of life, way of thinking and ethical behavior are so different from *ours* that neither nation has a good comprehension of the other. We need to understand that simply because a Russian's behavior may seem deceitful to us, it doesn't necessarily make him a bad person. He is only doing what he has been conditioned to do and what is expected of him in his society.

We must realize that nuclear weapons are impractical because they cannot be used without the risk of self-annihilation. We are obliged therefore to evaluate them not in relation to their use but rather in relation to the *threat* of their use. Being the chess player strategists they are, the Soviets were much quicker to realize this than the United States. By placing several of their chess men in Cuba they extracted from the United States a guaranteed sanctuary in the Western Hemisphere. By placing their SS-20 chess men on their western border, the Soviets doubtlessly hoped to dislodge the United States from Western Europe as they did in Cuba and in Eastern Europe. This

The Search for the Alternative

was glaringly revealed by the Russian negotiator, Mr. Kvitsinky, just before the Russians walked away from the arms control talks, when he told our Paul Nitze: "You have no business in Europe!"

To avoid living in a permanent state of jitters, the Western Europeans need a nuclear deterrent as much as does the United States. As stated by Andrei Sakharov, the famous Russian nuclear physicist, "If war is to be prevented, the United States must spend the billions that are necessary to provide the deterrent." So, even though the use of nuclear weapons is unthinkable and suicidal, for the present they are needed to offset Russian's threat to us and Western Europe.

CHAPTER III

Thoughtful Judgments

"One cool judgment is worth a thousand hasty councils."

— Woodrow Wilson

III

Thoughtful Judgments

1. There is a way to remove nuclear and other offensive, mass life-exterminating weapons, but it will not be accomplished by the kind of people, thinking and action that created the armament dilemma. Governments consist of power-oriented people. That's how they gain their position.

The decision and action to remove weapons of mass extermination will have to come from those who are free of the armament web: objective, realistic people who can see it for what it is and are free to act as they think.

2. They will have to make use of forces other than those used by the military, and employ them with strategy and discipline equal to or surpassing that used by the military.

3. There will be sacrifice, but not of life. There will be calculated risk, but not as much risk as now exists. There will be cost, but it will be a fraction of the present cost.

Thoughtful Judgments

4. To gain the support of the American people and the people of other nations with which the United States has substantial trade relations, the plan needs a sound foundation. It has to be built upon principles which all agree are just and equitable. Good administration will be imperative.

5. It will need to be a "stick and carrot" approach, rewarding those who do not commit or support aggression and through nonviolent means penalizing those who do.

6. The plan should be designed to divert talks with adversaries away from armament toward constructive,

mutually beneficial, common goals. Talking about armament is like fanning the wind, producing nothing except more wind.

7. It should be realistic and assume that in a lawless world each nation, regardless of what it says or agrees to do, is going to behave as it thinks necessary to protect itself from other nations.

8. It should not attempt to remake man, but rather accept him as he is, because there is little likelihood of eradicating the warrior in mankind's nature. Man's redeeming feature, as history shows, is that he will live peacefully

under law where there is effective and fair enforcement.

9. To reach the "Alternative World" we will need to build a structure. This we will call the "Alternative Plan." It will have to be a fully corrective plan, as halfway measures are of no value in solving a problem demanding a full fix.

10. If the plan does not effectively penalize aggresssion, it will continue to the point where all-out war between the superpowers is inevitable, and that would surely involve nuclear weapons.

11. The plan will have to be one that Russia can and will accept, at least eventually. It will have to provide her with benefits that are greater than can be obtained through aggression. It should be voluntary and offered as an invitation to join with us in ridding the earth of nuclear weapons and opposition to aggression which could lead to war.

12. Russians think and act differently than we, but let's quit calling them "enemies." They are just as human as we, and we have to learn to live with them; or if not, die with them.

13. We need to recognize that regardless

Thoughtful Judgments

of what they say or what agreements they sign, we can count on the Russians to do what they think is to their advantage. Our grand design should be to subtley open their eyes to what *is* to our mutual advantage.

14. **The only realistic refuge from the threat of nuclear war is in effective international law.** Even if nuclear weapons did not exist international law is going to be necessary to protect electric power plants (particularly nuclear power plants), oil and gas storage, pipelines, refineries, shipping and oil production platforms from destruction by terrorists.

15. While we are being realistic, let us

also face the fact that instruments of war produce nothing beneficial to mankind, rather they consume precious materials, human life and labor. Building arms and maintaining them diminishes mankind's quality of life and is a serious threat to his health. Economists agree that in the long run rather than increasing employment building arms creates unemployment.

16. The United States has repeatedly fought to preserve freedom in Western Europe, and would again. So that she does not misjudge us or the West Europeans, we must not allow Russia to forget this fact.

17. At present we are using our economic

power in the wrong way. This weakens our economy, prevents us from making desperately needed investments, heats up the arms race, offers no solution to the confrontation or hope of ever removing the threat of nuclear war.

18. The plan must be basically sound, feasible and simple, one that the average person can easily comprehend. Like the sword that cut through the mythical Gordian knot, it must be able to cut through the diplomatic tangle.

CHAPTER IV

The Alternative Defense Plan

"It is more difficult to organize peace than to win a war; but the fruits of victory will be lost if the peace is not well organized."

— *Aristotle*

IV

The Alternative Defense Plan

Using the ideas expressed in the previous chapter, "Thoughtful Judgments," we have designed what we call "The Alternative Defense Plan." It's an alternative to our government's present arms course. It's one we believe will reduce the chance of nuclear war in the near future and, eventually, possibly in 10 to 20 years, will offer the very real possibility of worldwide disarmament of all offensive weapons.

We have based the plan on the principles upon which the United States of America was founded, in the belief that these principles contain elements that have worldwide beneficial application. Our study indicates that the United States, with a wealth-creating economy and a political philosophy that supports individual human rights, has been less fervent in telling other people of the world about the fountainhead of these blessings than Russia has in telling people about its Marxism-Leninism theory that produces scarcity and serfdom. We find many Americans talk apologetically about the system that sustains them in freedom and plenty. If they are truly interested in helping other people, we know of

The Alternative Defense Plan

no better way than to tell them about our democracy and assist them in employing our economic system that produces plenty.

We believe, as did the founders of our nation, that people have certain inherent rights, that employers, governments, or any organization do not have the right to abridge. People are protected by law in our nation and in many others from having to work in an environment that endangers their health or life. Yet at the same time, there are many people in the USA and in many other nations contributing their labor, skill and inventiveness to making things just to kill people, possibly the very people that made them if they find their way into the hands of a nation that has no respect for these inherent rights.

Just before World War II we recall there

were protests against commercial interests selling scrap iron to Japan, but these were of no avail. As predicted, many American soldiers were killed with steel made in America. Today we hear those same voices saying, "We must continue trade with Russia on manufactured goods regardless of her military aggressiveness."

In a democratic society we expect quite a bit of different thought, but it is difficult for us to comprehend the logic of people who think it is all right for Russia to threaten Western Europe with her nuclear weapons but wrong for Western Europe to provide a deterrent to this threat. What is really more difficult yet is to comprehend the logic of people who think it is all right for Russia to maintain a military establishment in Cuba and export their aggression to other nations

The Alternative Defense Plan

in our backyard, but improper for us to help these nations defend themselves against this military aggression.

In the belief that wars of aggression are created by a small minority in governments, particularly in militaristic, dictatorial governments, we have designed our Alternative Defense Plan as an appeal to the majority of the people in all nations. Believing that the initiative and responsibility for establishing the plan must come from the United States — the origin of the nuclear arms problem — we have based the plan on the ideas of its founding fathers. We are presenting it in the form of a "Declaration" so that all may know where we stand as a people and as a nation.

Making Nuclear War Impossible

DECLARATION

We, the people of the United States, invite all people of the world who oppose military aggression and fear nuclear and other offensive, mass life-exterminating weapons to join with us in ceasing trade on all manufactured products (does not apply to earth products) with nations that use, threaten to use, or supply offensive weaponry, and any nation that trades directly or indirectly with such nations.

The Alternative Defense Plan

We see this "Declaration" as proclaiming an inherent right — the right to live, free from the fear of nuclear war.

To implement the Declaration we recommend that the United States establish an Alternative Agency (independent of but under the wing of the United Nations) which any nation can join, providing it meets with the terms of the Alternative. The Alternative Agency would be solely involved in activity pertaining to aggression and the use and supplying of offensive weaponry. Weapons that were judged to be purely defensive by the Alternative Enforcement Agency would be exempt.

We recommend that the terms of the Alternative Defense Plan contain these provisions: A nation declaring in favor of the Alternative Plan should discontinue the

Making Nuclear War Impossible

manufacture and supply of all offensive weaponry and withdraw all combat troops on foreign soil within one year from the date of making its Declaration. Not until this has been done should any nation be allowed to invoke the cessation of all trade on manufactured goods with aggressor and aggressor-supplying nations.

As stated in the Declaration, we do not propose cessation of trade on earth products such as oil, gas, minerals, metals and foods of all kinds. In fact, we would like to see international trade on these products increased. The withholding action, we believe, should be confined to man-made products because it is these that represent the threat. Earth products fall into an entirely different category. They are God-given.

Another reason for exempting earth

The Alternative Defense Plan

products is that the Alternative Defense Plan is designed to not unnecessarily penalize but to make a statement of position: not to make poorer but to make richer. Since Russia's greatest wealth is in natural resources, it could be that with very limited trade in manufactured goods she would build up a surplus of hard currency. To be able to spend this could be another inducement for joining the Alternative Alliance.

We propose that the Alternative Defense Plan use only voluntary and non-violent means to achieve its goals. All nations can choose whether or not to join with the United States in its Declaration against aggression and for freedom from mass life-exterminating weaponry. Nations making this Declaration would be required to

Making Nuclear War Impossible

register it with the Alternative Agency. In addition to its own surveillance over trade with aggressor and aggressor-related nations, it would be required to contribute to maintaining a trade-monitoring, investigative body. Its purpose would be to report to the Agency violations of the trade cessation agreement. Should a nation that had joined the Alternative Alliance of Nations be found in violation of the terms of the Alternative, it would be subject to economic sanctions, depending upon the seriousness of the violation. The sanctions should be sufficiently severe that no nation would knowingly violate the terms of the Alternative.

While the provisions of the Alternative call for the discontinuance of manufacture and supply of offensive weaponry one year

The Alternative Defense Plan

from date of Declaration, there is no prohibition for the Alternative-aligned nations against the possession and use **for defensive purposes** of offensive weapons that a nation has on hand at the time of suspension of trade. Neither is there any prohibition against the manufacture and sale of defensive weaponry or the use of advisors to help nations that are threatened militarily during the period of suspension of trade on manufactured goods.

It is expected that when, and if, two-thirds of the nations of the world, which would embody nations doing two-thirds or more of the world's international commerce (including Russia) have joined the non-aggression-aligned nations, the Alternative Defense Plan would become world law. It would have the authority over possession and use of offensive weapons and the responsibility for methodically destroying all offensive weapons on a pro-rata basis. Nations would keep only those weapons needed to maintain internal order and protect national boundaries. Since the kind of weapons permitted by persons or nations would be controlled by international law, it's conceivable that eventually nothing more lethal than a rifle might be the only legal weapon in the world.

AWF sees the Alternative Enforcement Agency as consisting of high-quality military personnel from possibly as many as a hundred nations. It would have power greater than any nation or group of nations.

Should any nation be concerned that this power might be unjustly turned against them, we ask: What greater security could

The Alternative Defense Plan

any nation have than the backing of two-thirds of the world's nations doing no less than two-thirds of the world's international commerce?

CHAPTER V

The Challenge

"There is no fate that plans men's lives. Whatever comes to us, good or bad, is usually the result of our own action or lack of action."

— Herbert N. Casson

V

The Challenge

Arnold Toynbee, in his book, *The Outline of History*, points out the part that challenge plays in the rise and fall of nations. Never in its 200 year history has the United States been challenged as it is today. Russia, our ally in the last World War, politically is challenging the cornerstones of our government and way of life. Militarily,

Making Nuclear War Impossible

Russia is challenging our international position. Japan, an adversary in the last World War, through her unique economic capability is challenging our position in world trade. Will the United States meet these challenges with imagination and set an example for other nations, or will it compromise its beliefs and ideals to the point where the mantle of leadership will fall to another? That is the question Americans have to answer. Both American management and labor have recognized the Japanese challenge and have made motions in the direction of competing with it. But they have yet to show the kind of imagination or put forth the effort to match, let alone surpass, the Japanese. Many seem to think that if they come close to the Japanese in quality and price that is good enough.

The Challenge

If only, we say to ourselves, most people in the United States were more fully aware of the situation and comprehended the magnitude of the challenge existing to the east and to the west of us, they would rise to the occasion to prove themselves equal to or better than those who challenge us. We know that the spirit, intelligence and energy to prove ourselves exists. It can be seen in most every corner of America. But we do not yet see the determination and national team spirit between management and labor we think necessary to meet the Japanese challenge, nor do we see in Congress the imagination and national spirit to meet the Russian challenge. The question is: Will the United States become a greater nation because of the challenges presented it, or will it not recognize its opportunities to lead other nations, by example, to a higher level of life?

We have great confidence in the youth of America. We think, today, we are developing one of the greatest generations in our existence as a nation. We believe that if we can bring to the youth of America the message that they can live and have children; that it isn't necessary for them to yield their lives to nuclear weapons, they will rise up and demand that their nation take definite action to rid the earth of these weapons. We do not believe they are going to cower to commercial interests or the fearful in the establishment who try to make us believe that taking a strong position against aggression and offensive weaponry is going to lead to war.

If we wish to continue to be a great na-

The Challenge

tion, let us embrace the wealth-creating challenge of the Japanese, and through a "stick and carrot" approach divert the death and destruction challenge of the Russians into channels that create wealth and a freer world society.

We don't want to delude anybody into believing that talking Russia into assigning her offensive armament to an international enforcement agency is going to be easy. It will probably be the most difficult selling job that the United States and the other Alternative-aligned nations have ever attempted. But, if pursued with conviction and a good understanding of the Russian mind, it can be done; for it offers Russia great benefits and takes nothing from her of value. It lifts from her back a very costly armament burden, gives her a guarantee

Making Nuclear War Impossible

against the threat of nuclear war, access to all free nation markets, equal status with any other nation, and does not threaten her Communist way of life.

CHAPTER VI

Victory Strategy

"In the advance of civilization, it is new knowledge which paves the way, and the pavement is eternal."

— *W. R. Whitney*

VI

Victory Strategy

The reason that the Declaration is addressed to the people of the world rather than to their governments is because we believe that it is extremely unlikely that any government (including our own) will have the courage to take a step bold enough to solve the arms dilemma without considerable pressure from its people. We believe it

Making Nuclear War Impossible

is imperative that nuclear arms and other mass life-exterminating weapons be made illegal worldwide, excepting what might be possessed by the Alternative International Police Authority.

The strategy behind (the provision of) discontinuing the manufacture and supplying of offensive weaponry one year after declaration is designed to break the armament logjam. It's what we refer to as the surgery or abnormal remedy to let all the world know that we are serious about our disarmament declaration and are willing to make the first meaningful move, but not a move that would put us at the mercy of an aggressor nation. This proposal assumes that we have sufficient offensive retaliatory capability at the time to deter an attack, and the capability of making defensive weapon-

Victory Strategy

ry that would counter present and new offensive weapons produced by an aggressor-oriented nation or nations.

We believe in the power of the people to change the thinking of their governments. We also see the use of economic power as a potent, nonviolent weapon.

Making Nuclear War Impossible

In 1921, Lenin wrote a memorandum that read as follows:

They (the capitalist nations) will supply us with the materials and the technology which we lack, and will restore our military industry which we need for our future attacks upon our suppliers. In other words, they will work hard in order to prepare their suicide.

Victory Strategy

Later Lenin said that the capitalist nations will sell them the rope we will use to hang them. In simple terms, what we are proposing is to quit selling people rope for our hanging. The Russians have followed Lenin almost to the letter. With the help of the rope that the western nations have provided them, they have built the largest military machine on earth. They have used it effectively to subject other nations and increase their sphere of influence.

If the United States has the courage to take a firm stand on not selling rope (manufactured goods) to nations guilty of aggression or those supporting such nations, it can put the brakes on and eventually stop aggression. By courage we mean standing solidly for what we believe. It also means willingness to take a calculated risk, to make some sacrifice, and impose self-discipline. Whenever this is mentioned, the freeloaders raise their voices. They don't seem to realize that anything of great value cannot be obtained without price. But who, if infected with a deadly cancer, which is the condition of our world body, would value their money more than their life? The problem we face is apathy. Most people think it might happen to somebody else but not to them. Facing reality — looking death in the face — is difficult; but do it we must to survive.

Russia has the same choice as every other nation. If it chooses aggression, it should pay the cost. Should it choose nonaggression, there would be no prohibition of trade in manufactured goods. It's entirely up to her. But it's also up to us. If we do not

Victory Strategy

approve of aggression and believe it will lead to war, then we shouldn't support it in any way.

Assuming that the government of the United States made the Declaration we propose, how would the other nations react? It's our opinion that a few — very few — would applaud us. Some would try gentle persuasion to get us to reverse our stand, and a lot would scream that they were being denied their rights. In the United States people have the right to trade what they wish and with whom they wish. This is true in most nations. But considering that some are tied into contracts of one kind or another, the United States should in advance of making its Declaration let all nations read it and have a chance to meet their short-term contracts. But it should also convince all nations that it is fully dedicated to its Declaration.

If the United States stands firm on its Declaration and does not sell any manufactured goods to nations engaging in aggression or any nation trading with a nation engaging in aggression, we believe the following scenario will result. The great majority of the free industrialized nations of the world will eventually join the United States in the Alternative Alliance. At first there will be some holdouts. But through gentle persuasion and the pressure of economics, they will eventually join in the crusade to abolish nuclear weapons. Since there is no prohibition on trade of earth products and Russia has little to offer in manufactured goods, we expect that those who choose Russia for their manufactured

Victory Strategy

goods trading partner over the United States and other Alternative-aligned nations will not be large in international trade and few in number.

When the Alternative Alliance becomes reality and a majority of the nations have joined it and others are on the brink of joining, we expect Russia will become very vocal and try to convince holdout nations that she is being cornered and coerced by the United States. She probably will threaten war, spout a lot of venomous talk, make calculated warlike gestures, but will stop short of actual war.

Some fear that Russia might react to a trade sanction by declaring war. This is highly improbable. Unlike our war policy which is reactionary, Russia's is a long-term design. Going to war over a trade sanction would be contrary to this design and past behavior.

Moreover, she is too vulnerable and has too much to lose to risk war against formidable enemies. Lenin told them, and he has been right most of the time, that capitalist nations because of their greed for money will carry on commerce at any cost. Realizing the fragility of national alliances and the ineffectiveness of most previous boycotts, she will never believe that the Alternative Alliance will hold together. And she has been too successful in circumventing boycotts in the past to feel threatened.

But assuming that the great majority of the free industrialized nations do hold together, (and this will be primarily dependent upon the will and self-discipline of the United States) the flow of manufactured goods and technology from them would probably be reduced to a trickle. Then Russia, with a per capita income well below the average of the free industrialized nations, will get increasingly further behind the longer she holds out. Likewise, the nations under Russia's control will eventually feel the pinch if they are not able to trade with the free industrialized nations. This could put the brakes on establishing further beachheads through aggression.

What about the Eastern European nations that are quite highly industrialized, and Russia herself? Won't they be able to carry on and support themselves and the other nations under Russian domination on a comparable basis to the West? They probably could if they had a free, competitive, economic system; but under the Communist

Making Nuclear War Impossible

Russian, totalitarian, economic system, and without the support of the free industrialized nations, it would be next to impossible. The reason for this is in one word: competition. Without it no economic system can be highly productive. Even with all the financial help and technology that the western nations have given to Russia and her satellites, except for producing a mammoth war machine, she has accomplished nothing in the field of manufacturing worthy of note.

We estimate that in 10 to 15 years without the support of the free industrialized nations the difference in the standard of living in Russia and in her trading partners compared to that in the Alternative-aligned nations will be so great and so evident that Russia will want to seriously consider joining the Alternative Alliance. It could be that she would join much earlier if the Alternative-aligned nations employ what we call the "friendship offensive." It's basically an attitude that would prompt the nations in the Alternative Alliance to tell Russia, when appropriate, that we sincerely would like to have you with us, and demonstrate the advantages. The "friendship offensive" is an effort to step up exchange in all areas except manufactured goods. It's a willingness to understand how difficult change is for Russia. But it's also a willingness to stand absolutely solid against aggression and possession of mass life-exterminating weapons.

The United States should keenly feel its responsibility in helping to eliminate aggression. It was the United States that encouraged Russia on this road of aggression. By

Making Nuclear War Impossible

forsaking its beliefs at the end of World War II, transferring territorial rights into the hands of a despot heading a tyrannical form of government as bad as the one just defeated, the United States told all the world that it was not committed to its beliefs excepting as it applied to its own people, and that it was willing to sacrifice the rights of others when it was expedient and served its self-interest.

We had the power at the end of World War II to insist that the innocent nations caught in the war between Germany and Russia be given their freedom, but we lacked the courage and will to use it. Had we finished the job, seeing to it that all European nations that had been run over by Germany were given their freedom, it's possible we wouldn't have the confronta-

Victory Strategy

tion with Russia that we have today. We accepted Russia's position that because she had crossed over the Eastern European nations to get at the heart of Germany, they belonged to her, which was all wrong. Conquest was not the reason for fighting the war.

It didn't take Russia long to comprehend that the United States was not fully committed to its beliefs, and they could, with impunity, force their tyrannical rule over other nations. This they did in Hungary, Czechoslovakia and all of the Eastern European nations to which the United States had already given consent, and in more recent years, Afghanistan. We believe that in bowing to tyranny and aggression we gave Russia a false image of ourself, sinned against our forefathers and sowed the seeds

Making Nuclear War Impossible

of World War III, which will be the result if aggression is not brought to a halt.

We can guess, but, of course, we don't have any way of knowing what Russia's reaction would be to our Declaration. Being our adversary, she probably will think it a design against her. And should she think this way, we will have to take the time and patience to explain that this is not so. We will have to try to convince her that our unilateral action is directed toward relieving the world from the threat of nuclear weapons and aggression that we fear might lead to war between our two great nations, and a war which we view as totally unnecessary and self-destructive.

We are aware of the desire to go for a quick solution, but we don't believe a quick solution can achieve worthwhile, lasting results. Any solution that gives only temporary relief may well be worse than none at all. It could lead people into believing that the problem had been solved when all we did was stick our heads in the sand. To solve a problem we must be willing to look it straight in the eye. The confrontation between the USA and USSR has been long in building. It has assumed tremendous proportions. It is going to take time, patience, understanding, and a determined effort to reduce it to a comfortable level.

We believe that appeasement eventually leads to war. For nations, people, and many forms of animal life, boundaries are necessary for peaceful co-existence. When aggression occurs, fighting follows. Internally, nations establish laws that penalize people who violate the rights of others, but, externally, nations can indulge in aggression against other nations, because we live in a lawless world and there is no penalty other than the loss of life that results in the fighting and the material cost. **The essence of the "Alternative Defense Plan" is to make aggression so unprofitable through the prudent and strategic use of economic power that no nation will consider its use.**

With the ending of aggression, we believe that the formerly aggressive nations will turn from creating machines of destruction to producing things that will help people live **a more** abundant life. In support of this, **we cite the** example of Japan. Defeated in an all-out effort to conquer with military might, Japan turned to making products for people. It was here that she found her true power and glory, and through it has con-

Victory Strategy

quered the world in a way unimaginable with military power. "Conquering" the world through commerce has brought prosperity to the Japanese people and international respect to her nation. Today, her yen is one of the most valued currencies. At the same time, she has provided people throughout the world with valuable products, things that they want and need. And she has done all of this without sacrifice to her people.

If any doubt exists that war is not the way, let us, by contrast, consider Russia. Victorious in war she has continued to pursue her god through war. Today, she sits on a mountain of military junk. Her people live in want and slavery. Scarcity, deceit and suspicion stalk her land and every nation on which she has laid her imperialistic hand.

Making Nuclear War Impossible

She manufactures few goods acceptable to the world market. Her ruble has no international value. Feared by all nations, she continues to infect the weak ones with her paranoid war ways through the use of the gun. What an opportunity for the United States to use its economic power, combined with that of other free industrialized nations, to bring Russia to a realization that the war way does not pay. She probably is not going to accept this, at least not immediately, for she is still too enamored with her mammoth war machine and still believes she is going to conquer us and other capitalist nations through military force. We must make her understand that we will never yield to her if it means fighting to the last man; and if she takes us on, she can expect a war to the death.

Victory Strategy

It's possible that Russia will not turn from her aggressive ways until she has a freer society. People kept in confinement behind walls, not permitted to travel outside of their nation, people denied ownership of property, people denied the opportunity to exploit their creativeness and energy other than through government prescribed rules of order, become frustrated. Frustration can lead to aggressiveness, and this could be a Russian characteristic for some time. Our job, as we see it now, is to man the ramparts until Russia turns from her present war way.

Until that day arrives let us try with a supreme effort to divert attention in our talks with the Russians from things that destroy man to things that will help him live a fuller, healthier life.

Making Nuclear War Impossible

We believe that eventually there will be a loosening of some of the chains that bind the people in the Communist, totalitarian-controlled states. And with a greater degree of freedom, we expect there will be a greater degree of interest on the part of the bureaucratic rulers to seriously consider assigning their offensive weapons to the Alternative World Agency in exchange for complete economic freedom and freedom from the threat of nuclear war.

The ultimate goal of the Alternative World Plan is effective international law, with authority over all weapons that are classified by the Alternative Agency as offensive. The only truly offensive weapons in existence in the world would be those under the control of the Alternative Enforcement Agency.

Victory Strategy

Today we live in a lawless world. This condition cannot long exist. Lawlessness, because of its nature, has always had to yield to law and authority. We are standing before the Judge of time and history, trying to make up our minds whether to yield our offensive weapons to international law and enforcement or whether to let international war make the decision for us.

Let us not deceive ourselves by putting faith in treaties, for in a lawless world treaties are just another form of war. It has been the common practice among nations to use negotiations and treaties to hide their real intentions. Increased negotiations have been the customary prelude to war. In every case during the last World War the aggressor nation used negotiations and treaties to anesthetize its intended victim before launching its military attack. Even the wary Stalin was taken in by Hitler with this soothing tactic, so much so that although he was told by the British and others that Hitler was planning an invasion of Russia, Stalin did not believe it until it happened.

CHAPTER VII

Life Assurance

"The Alternative Life Assurance Plan is an exchange of national sovereignty over devastating offensive weapons for international protection from such weapons."
— *Howard Brembeck*

VII

Life Assurance

The world in which we now are living is depending upon MAD, the acronym for Mutual Assured Destruction, to prevent nuclear war. The Alternative World Plan proposes MAS, Mutual Assured Survival. Our present world proposes reduction or control of nuclear weapons but offers no realistic plan for control. The Alternative

Making Nuclear War Impossible

World proposes complete elimination of nuclear weapons and a feasible plan for protection against further manufacture of such weapons.

The present world plan, even if it were successful beyond all expectations and reduced the amount of nuclear arms in existence by fifty percent or even ninety percent, would still leave enough nuclear weapons remaining to destroy every large city in the United States and Russia. To think that it is possible to control nuclear weapons and still permit nations to possess them we believe is an illusion. As long as nuclear weapons exist under the control of any nation, they will continue to endanger the lives of millions of people. Ironically, if this monster, instead of being a nuclear weapon under the control of the military of

Life Assurance

individual nations, was a deadly virus of plague proportions that threatened to take the lives of millions of people throughout the world, all nations would converge on the United Nations and demand that they take whatever steps were necessary to eradicate the plague. There would be no thought of national sovereignty, only concern for human life.

The Alternative World Plan is much more than assured survival. It offers life at a higher level, economically, aesthetically, and socially. It offers freedoms and opportunities for mankind that do not exist in our present world.

CHAPTER VIII

The Land Of The Free And The Home Of The Brave

"Be courageous! Be as brave as your fathers before you. Have faith! Go forward."
— Thomas Edison
last public message

VIII

The Land Of The Free And The Home Of The Brave

In writing our national anthem, Francis Scott Key closely connected the words "Free" and "Brave." This, we feel, has special significance for our time. We are being challenged by an immoral government. It is challenging us to defend the basic principles upon which our nation was founded, principles which have sustained it

Making Nuclear War Impossible

for over 200 years, principles that have made it the world leader, the fountainhead of industry, new ideas and freedom.

The bravery that we feel is needed in the United States now, if we are to remain a free nation and avoid the catastrophe of war, is not the bravery to die, but the bravery to live for the freedoms which we inherited from those who established our nation and those who have preserved them for us, often at the sacrifice of their lives. We should leave no doubt in the minds of Russia's rulers that this is the foundation upon which we stand and from which we will not be moved. If we stand united, they will respect us. From time to time they will test our resolve. If we answer with firmness, then our children and our children's children can also have life, and, like us, will be

The Land of the Free and The Home of the Brave

able to sing . . . THE LAND OF THE FREE AND THE HOME OF THE BRAVE!

CHAPTER IX

Living In The Alternative World

*"The empires of the future
are empires of the mind."*
— *Winston Churchill*

IX

Living In The Alternative World

Living in the Alternative World — a world wherein the fear of death from nuclear arms does not exist, a world where all the effort and resources presently spent for killing people are spent to enhance life and further exploration into the secrets of the earth and the universe — cannot yet be fully comprehended. So much of our wealth,

Making Nuclear War Impossible

energy and technical ability is required by the military that we don't know what would happen if all of this was spent to create rather than to destroy.

We hear voices hailing the Alternative World Plan as the Magna Charta of the common people from the serfdom of armament and war. Finally, at last we hear them say, "It is now impossible for the would-be Hitlers to create armies of aggression."

Still dreaming of the grandeur of a world without armament and war, we are awakened to our senses by someone who says, "There's a gulf between our world and the Alternative World. To cross it we will need a sturdy ship and good hands; for the waters are turbulent and it will take years to reach the shore of the Alternative World." Many become frightened. Others are discouraged

Living in The Alternative World

because it's going to be such a long trip. Many don't believe that the ship is properly designed or is built sturdy enough to make the trip. Some don't have confidence in the officers and crew that will be manning the ship. But we who have faith in ourselves recall there were people who said the same about the Mayflower.

The ship to which we refer is the "Alternative Defense Years," necessary to bring Russia to a realization that aggression is unprofitable and that international control of offensive weapons would be to her advantage. Many people use the argument that such a ship cannot be built and successfully cross the gulf to the Alternative World simply because it has never been done. It just won't work. What they should have said and what they all know to be true is that it hasn't been done because nobody has done it, or it hasn't worked because nobody has made it work. Not many years ago the whole Western Hemisphere of our earth didn't exist for the people of the Eastern Hemisphere. Just a few years ago ninety-nine percent of the people on earth would have said that it's impossible to go to the moon. Nobody has, therefore, nobody can.

The question we have for the people who have created the greatest nation on earth, who have led all other nations in discoveries, ideas, who have walked on the moon and sent spaceships to the farthest reaches of our solar system is: **"Have we become so impotent, so faithless, that we cannot do, or do not have the will to do, what we know must be done?"**

> "The only thing necessary
> for evil to triumph
> is for good men to do nothing."
> — Edmond Burke